KEEPING
lizards

A PRACTICAL GUIDE TO
CARING FOR UNUSUAL PETS

DAVID MANNING

First edition for the United States, Canada, and the Philippine
Republic published by Barron's Educational Series, Inc., 2000.

Originally published in English by
HarperCollins*Publishers* Ltd under the title:
COLLINS UNUSUAL PETS: KEEPING CREEPY CRAWLIES
Text and design © HarperCollins*Publishers* Ltd, 2000
Photographs © David Manning, 2000
Illustrations © Felicity Rose Cole, 2000

David Manning asserts the moral right to be identified as the
author of this work.

All inquiries should be addressed to:
Barron's Educational Series, Inc.
250 Wireless Boulevard
Hauppauge, New York 11788
http://www.barronseduc.com

Library of Congress Catalog Card No. 99-69420

International Standard Book No. 0-7641-1281-3

9 8 7 6 5 4 3 2 1

Designer: Colin Brown
Photography: Animal Ark, London
Illustrations: Felicity Rose Cole

Color reproduction by Colourscan, Singapore
Printed and bound by Printing Express Ltd, Hong Kong

Please Note
While every reasonable care was taken in the compilation of
this publication, the Publisher and Author cannot accept
liability for any loss, damage, injury, or death resulting from
the keeping of lizards by user(s) of this publication, or
from the use of any materials, equipment, methods, or
information recommended in this publication or from any
errors or omissions that may be found in the text of this
publication or that may occur at a future date, except as
expressly provided by law.

Contents

Introduction

Reptiles, especially lizards, are becoming an increasingly popular choice of pet. I would describe them as low-maintenance pets. Many lizards require only occasional feeding and cleaning, and none require walks, annual injections, or grooming. Other major benefits are that lizards will not affect asthmatics, make little or no noise, and can be kept in homes where space is limited.

This book will help you to select a lizard suitable for you and your particular circumstances. The different species are organized in an ease-of-care order. The easiest to keep appear first, graduating to those that are more demanding in terms of equipment, space, and maintenance time.

Choosing a pet

There are several factors you need to consider when choosing a pet lizard. You have to decide on the space you have available at home, what you are prepared to feed your lizard, and whether you wish to handle your pet frequently or only occasionally. This book will help guide you in the right direction.

Space requirements

The size of the accommodation required depends on the lizard's size, age, the number you are keeping together, and their habitat. The following information gives an indication of space requirements for each species.

Small: day geckos, Green Anole, Leopard Gecko (individuals only).

Medium: day geckos in groups, Green Anoles in groups, Leopard Geckos in groups, Bearded Dragon, Blue-tongued Skink, Uromastyx, Plumed Basilisk.

Large: Green Iguana, chameleons, Savannah Monitor, Water Dragon.

Handling

The frequency with which you are able to handle your lizard will depend upon the species and the amount of time you are prepared to put in to tame it while it is still young. Providing your lizard with food treats while handling may help you to tame it. Some lizards, however, are best enjoyed for their beauty and behavior and are not suitable for handling on a regular basis. See the list below to determine which lizard is best for you.

Regular: Leopard Gecko, Bearded Dragon, Blue-tongued Skink.

Occasional: Green Iguana, Water Dragon, Uromastyx, Savannah Monitor, chameleons.

Rare: day geckos, Plumed Basilisk, Green Anole.

Diet

The food you are prepared to feed your pet will, in some part, determine your choice of lizard. If you really do not like the thought of feeding your lizard live bugs and pink mice, you may prefer to buy a pet that only eats plant matter. Lizard diets are divided into 4 categories. Herbivores eat only plant matter, omnivores consume plants and animals, and insectivores tend to eat mainly insects. A very few large lizards are carnivores and eat other animals.

In general lizards are easy to keep and clean, and they make attractive pets. A few of the species available in the pet trade are captive bred.

Herbivore: Uromastyx, Green Iguana.

Omnivore: Blue-tongued Skink, Bearded Dragon, Veiled Chameleon, Water Dragon.

Insectivore: Green Anole, day geckos (with nectar), Leopard Gecko, Plumed Basilisk (with vegetables), Panther Chameleon, Savannah Monitor.

Where to obtain stock?

Once you have decided to keep a lizard it is necessary to locate a good source of livestock, and the equipment and foods that you need to maintain your pet.

Approaching a breeder for your pet may be helpful, but only a pet store or mail order company is likely to offer the range of equipment, vivaria, and foods required to maintain your pet over a long period of time. Herpetological societies, reptile and pet care magazines, and the Internet should help you to locate good local sources.

Selecting a healthy individual

If possible, choose a captive-bred animal that is already feeding well. You obviously want to select a healthy individual to begin with and the following information will help you to pick the most healthy lizard.

Look for specimens:
- that are bright-eyed and alert-looking
- that do not bolt or flee
- that are good feeders
- with straight limbs – no kinks or twists in the bone structure

Avoid specimens:
- that have a dirty vent – caked-on fecal matter is a sure sign of problems
- that lie listlessly on the floor of the cage
- that are too small or the runt of the litter
- that cannot support their own weight or that walk in an uncomfortable manner
- with very little fat reserves around the base of the tail

Captive-bred lizards

Purchasing lizards from captive-bred stocks helps to ensure that they are free from internal or external parasites. Some imported specimens can be more difficult to maintain and are not as parasite-free as captive-bred specimens. Wild-caught lizards may also take some time to adapt to their new homes.

Home breeding

It is beyond the scope of this book to go into details on how to breed lizards. Much information can be found by joining a herpetological society or from other reference books. It is essential to keep a mature pair/small group of lizards before breeding can be attempted, and if successful, it is a thrilling and fascinating achievement. Newly hatched lizards require considerable care to enable them to thrive, so nurturing baby lizards encourages a respect for life and shows that you are responsible in caring for a dependent animal.

This Leopard Gecko is active and alert because it is healthy.

KEY

In the species pages, each icon shows at a glance the keeping requirements and basic facts that will influence your choice of pet. This is general information only and more detailed requirements are given in the text.

Accommodation

This symbol indicates the type of home each species requires. There are 4 basic types: desert terrestrial, tropical terrestrial, desert arboreal, and tropical arboreal.

Diet

The lizards have one of the following diets: herbivorous, omnivorous, or insectivorous. Any variations to these diets are discussed in the main text.

Maximum Life Span

This information gives a rough idea of a lizard's life span in captivity. Many factors, from poor diet to breeding strain, can shorten their life expectancy.

Maximum Length

The maximum length of an individual lizard is given for males only. In general, females tend to be smaller than males.

This young monitor lizard is warming itself on a hand.

Anatomy

All lizards are reptiles and, like humans, they are vertebrate animals that have a skull, backbone, and ribs. They are classified by scientists into the suborder Sauria. Among the 3,000 species of discovered lizards there are considerable differences in size, shape, and lifestyle. They are, however, bound together by common characteristics.

External features

Skin
The scaly skin is a protective outer covering that helps prevent a lizard from dehydrating. Scale formation varies from species to species, while special pigment-bearing cells called chromatophores enable some species to change color when necessary. Many species have distinct markings while still young.

Tongue
In most lizards the tongue is short and thick, but is notably long in chameleons and forked in monitors. The tongue works in conjunction with the Jacobson's organ. This remarkable structure, located in the mouth, analyzes or "tastes" whatever the tongue comes into contact with.

Ears
Most lizards have a visible external ear opening, sometimes covered by a tympanum (ear drum).

Eyes
Unlike snakes, which have no moveable eyelids, most lizards have eyelids. Special adaptations include the chameleon's independently moving eyes and the gecko's large eyes to aid night vision. A few burrowing lizards are eyeless.

Limbs
Limbs are specialized organs, and the fingers and toes are adapted according to the habitat and lifestyle of each species. For example, most geckos and all

anoles have adhesive pads near the tips of their digits to enable them to climb smooth surfaces such as ceilings and walls.

Tail

Tails are useful tools and, depending on the species, may be used for grasping, balancing, and storage of fatty deposits. Tails may be shed as a means of defense to distract potential predators. Never pick up your lizard by the tail. Tails can also be used in defense like a stout whip.

Internal organs

Lizards are equipped with organs similar to those of mammals. The skull encases a brain and lizards breathe air into lungs just like humans. A liver removes toxins and the alimentary canal processes food.

Thermoregulation

Lizards are reliant totally on external conditions for survival. Unlike mammals, they do not possess the ability to generate internal heat. Lizards are, therefore, called cold-blooded or ectothermic.

Lizards warm up and cool down (thermoregulate) by moving around their environment. On a cool morning they seek out the sun's rays – or the heating pad or spotlight in a vivarium – to bask in the warmth to recharge their batteries.

Once they reach their optimum temperature, they can move around quite rapidly and look for food, patrol their territory, and get on with their daily lives. On hot days they must avoid fatal overheating by resting in the shade, cooling off in the water, or seeking the coolness of a burrow or retreat.

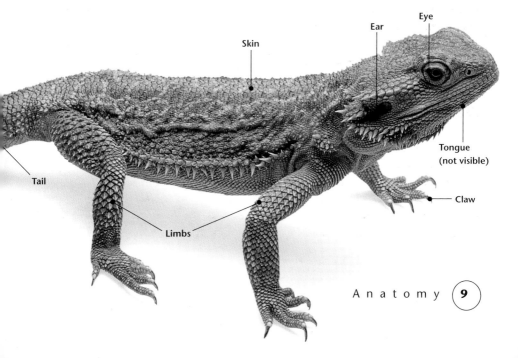

Skin

Ear

Eye

Tongue
(not visible)

Tail

Claw

Limbs

Caging

For the long-term care and health of your pet lizards it is essential that the correct environment – in terms of heat, light, and space – is created and all their needs are met.

The start-up costs of buying vivaria or cages and equipment may be relatively high compared to the actual cost of your lizard, but it is always better to buy the best-quality equipment that you can afford because it will last a long time and will help you to create the right environment for your pet lizard.

Time and effort spent on preparing caging will also bring rewards for you as you will enjoy viewing your lizard in its new home.

Your choice of lizard will determine what equipment is required to establish and maintain the correct conditions. Make sure the right amount of heat, light, and humidity are available for your pet. As long as a lizard's basic needs are met, they are unaware of how simple or elaborate the decoration is in their cage or vivarium.

Containers

There are three main types of vivaria.
Wood Wooden or plywood vivaria have sliding glass doors and a ventilation mesh to allow good movement of air.
Plastic These containers are particularly good for storing live foods and raising baby lizards. They tend to be inexpensive, but few are sturdy enough for larger lizards. It is unsafe to attach ceramic heaters or lights to plastic containers but they are ideal for species that require only a heating pad.
Glass This is the best option for housing. They can be made in any size, are easy to clean, and are probably the most attractive option for housing small- to medium-sized pet lizards.

The required dimensions of a vivarium are determined by the size of lizard, its

This inexpensive and easy-to-clean type of caging is available in a range of sizes from most pet stores.

| Lighting options | Ceramic heater | Heater pad | Thermostat |

age, the numbers you are to keep together, and their habit requirements. Throughout this book vivarium dimensions are given as length x height x width.

Lighting and heating

Special equipment is readily available to provide light and heat for pet lizards.

Fluorescent/full-spectrum lights These provide essential ultraviolet light (UVA and UVB) with minimal heat. This sort of light is beneficial and often essential for lizards that need to bask – it enables them to absorb calcium, which is necessary for healthy bone development.

Light bulbs These are useful for heating and lighting, but have no UVA content. Animals and furnishings should be protected from coming into direct contact with them.

Spotlights These are most useful for providing direct heat and light to a basking area.

Ceramic heaters and infrared bulbs Powerful heaters especially good for nighttime heating. They provide no light

and they must be thermostatically controlled. Animals and keepers must be protected from contact with them.

Heating pads Low, medium, and high wattage heating pads are available. Never cover more than half the ground area in the vivarium with a heating pad. Higher wattage pads need controlling with a thermostat and all pads need regular checking as their effectiveness can deteriorate over time.

Thermostat The temperature of all heaters and lights should be regulated with an appropriate thermostat.

Thermometer All vivaria benefit from one or more thermometers to accurately measure temperature.

Temperature gradients

It is very important to provide the correct range of temperatures within a vivarium to enable lizards to warm up and cool down as necessary. This is called a temperature gradient. To achieve this you simply place the major heat source toward one end of the vivarium. By regulating its output with a thermostat and monitoring the temperature with a thermometer you can achieve the hot end of the gradient scale. Measure the temperature at the other end of the vivarium and you should have achieved the right type of gradient.

Water

Lizards require fresh water, which should be available in a clean bowl. Ideally, sink a suitably-sized water dish into the substrate so that it can be accessed easily for both drinking and bathing. Larger lizards will require a large bowl or tub which cannot be turned over. Some lizards prefer to drink from water droplets, so mist spraying is essential. Mist spraying is also needed to maintain humidity levels in some setups. However, you must ensure that your vivarium is adequately ventilated so that the air does not stagnate.

Species that prefer a drier environment benefit from and use humid areas. A pile of plastic plants or an upturned plastic box filled with moss or vermiculite and sprayed regularly with water will create a humid microclimate. All species enjoy a good mist spray and it is particularly beneficial when they are shedding skin. A hygrometer can be used to measure humidity.

Hygrometer

The water feature is a recent innovation. This is, in effect, a small pond with the added benefit of a pump circulating water over a rock-type background.

Substrates

A large variety of substrates are available to cover the base of your vivarium, and your choice will depend on the needs of your pet and your aesthetic preferences. Many breeders keep lizards in bare setups with only newspaper as a base. This does not affect the happiness of a lizard, but I prefer more natural displays that incorporate a mixture of substrates and furnishings.

Play sand and gravel These are useful for desert species.

Wood and bark chips Avoid the finest types because particles taken in with foods cause digestive problems.

Leaf litter Leaves and pine cones, etc., enhance the look of a vivarium. These are best frozen overnight to kill pests.

Reptile grass This green matting is easily washed and very versatile.

Paper This is easy to clean and replace.

Shelters

Shelters are invaluable for giving lizards a sense of security. Rocks, wood, cork bark, and plastic plants can all provide retreats for your pet lizard, and it is better to have too many than too few shelters.

Furnishings

Naturalistic backgrounds, driftwood, cork bark, real, plastic, and silk plants, can all be used to make your vivarium more attractive. Manufactured furnishings can be easier to clean than natural ones. A wide range are now available at most pet stores.

Setups

The lizards in this book require 4 different types of accommodation based on the habitats they are found in. With slight variations in temperature and humidity levels the following setups are suitable for most lizards and cover the critical factors of heat, light, shelter, and moisture. It is by variation of these factors that most lizards can be accommodated. However, these setups are designed for guidance only, and for precise details of how to create the correct environment for your lizard, please read the relevant text for each species.

Tropical arboreal

This setup is suitable for lizards that need height and high humidity levels. Climbing lizards enjoy height and appropriate-sized logs or branches to climb and bask on. Panther Chameleons and iguanas appreciate more height, while Water Dragons and Plumed Basilisks are more interested in the overall area available to move around in and a good vantage point over water. If keeping a community of lizards, it is advisable to offer a couple of basking areas and lots of cover.

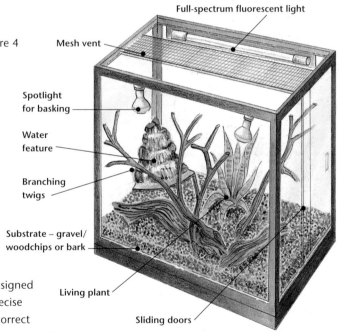

Full-spectrum fluorescent light

Mesh vent

Spotlight for basking

Water feature

Branching twigs

Substrate – gravel/ woodchips or bark

Living plant

Sliding doors

All-glass vivarium for tropical arboreal setup

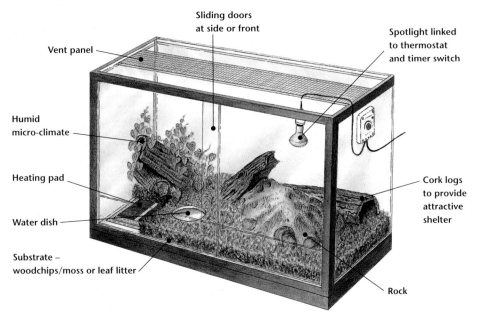

Sliding doors at side or front

Spotlight linked to thermostat and timer switch

Vent panel

Humid micro-climate

Heating pad

Water dish

Substrate – woodchips/moss or leaf litter

Cork logs to provide attractive shelter

Rock

All-glass vivarium for tropical terrestrial setup

Tropical terrestrial

This setup is suitable for ground-dwelling lizards that require high humidity levels. Non-basking species do not necessarily require a spotlight, but would benefit from an additional heating pad. Sturdy rocks and chunky decorations are suitable – anything too delicate will be trampled on. Keep a moist area toward one end of the vivarium but mist spray throughout to maintain overall humidity levels.

Desert terrestrial

This setup is ideal for ground-dwelling species that need hot and dry conditions. Leopard Geckos are simply accommodated in any warm place and a heating pad suffices. The basking Uromastyx, however, needs a rock upon which to sit and soak up the bright light and heat. Both species like logs or burrows for shelter, and a humid area and occasional spraying will keep their environment fresh but dry. Substrates like sand and gravel are best disposed of and replaced periodically for good hygiene.

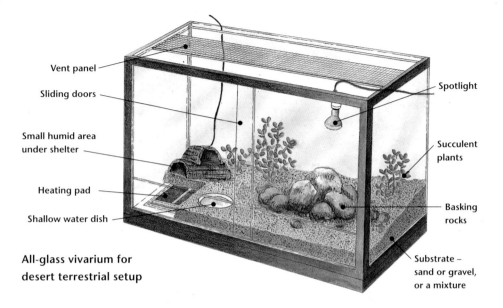

Vent panel

Sliding doors

Small humid area
under shelter

Heating pad

Shallow water dish

Spotlight

Succulent
plants

Basking
rocks

**All-glass vivarium for
desert terrestrial setup**

Substrate –
sand or gravel,
or a mixture

Desert arboreal

This setup is best for species that live above ground and prefer hot and dry temperatures. Without "cooking" your lizard, a desert environment should be both dry and hot. At least one cooler area, shelter or cave, should be available, allowing the lizards to thermoregulate.

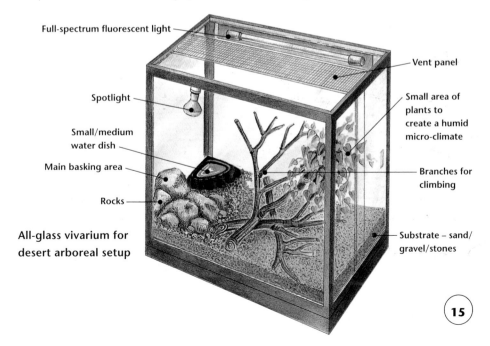

Full-spectrum fluorescent light

Spotlight

Small/medium
water dish

Main basking area

Rocks

Vent panel

Small area of
plants to
create a humid
micro-climate

Branches for
climbing

**All-glass vivarium for
desert arboreal setup**

Substrate – sand/
gravel/stones

Feeding

All lizards need food to enable them to develop and thrive. The amount and type of food required and the frequency of feeding will vary depending on the type, size, and age of the lizard. It is essential to establish a good feeding regime, and to prepare and store foods under hygienic conditions. Fresh water is vital for most species, and many lizards enjoy a bath or mist spray within their vivarium.

Most lizards are predators, which means they hunt for and eat anything they can catch. Generally, insects are the most abundant foods found in lizard habitats.

The lizard diet can be divided into four categories. Herbivores only eat plants and fruits. Insectivores feed only on insects, while carnivores only feed on other animals. Omnivores are less specific and will eat all types of foods, including plants, animals, and insects.

HERBIVORES

A large range of suitable fruits and vegetables can be purchased at grocery stores or grown in pesticide-free gardens or allotments. The most popular foods include: romaine lettuce, broccoli, tomato, pear, apple, edible berries, dandelion leaves and flowers, green beans, grated carrot, cooked potato, cabbage, flowers, and almost any nonpoisonous leaves or

Juveniles and older lizards will benefit from having some of their greens chopped or shredded.

weeds. Wherever you live, and depending on the season, a vast range of suitable foods will be available to collect or buy locally. Utilize these foods when you are able – most reptiles love and benefit from the natural sugars, vitamins, and minerals they contain.

Daily feedings are the best way to satisfy the nutritional needs of herbivores and omnivores. Large species, such as iguanas, can eat coarsely chopped pears and apples, whereas smaller lizards require their food more finely chopped or diced.

Food should be provided on shallow

The Uromastyx is totally herbivorous. It feeds mainly on green leaf foods but it will also eat fruit and vegetables.

trays away from main basking spots so that it does not dry out. Remove uneaten foods the day after feeding to minimize fouling.

INSECTIVORES

Most lizards, and the majority of species covered in this book, are insectivores. They feed on a wide range of invertebrates, such as insects and spiders.

Stalking live prey helps to keep pet lizards occupied and fit. However, do not leave too many live bugs in the vivarium because they may hassle an overfed lizard. Lizards will also enjoy jumping around after household pests like flies and spiders. These can be an extra source of protein as well as a treat for your pet.

Do take care when collecting your own insect foods for you pet because you may run the risk of introducing some unwanted vivarium pests. However, the benefit of wild-caught live foods is that they are filled with naturally acquired vitamins and minerals.

A variety of commercially bred insects, and some processed whole foods, are widely available through pet stores and mail order. Remember to maintain your live foods in good condition and ensure they are well fed and cared for. Small plastic pet homes are useful storage containers. Insectivores will enjoy a selection of the following live foods, listed in order of size.

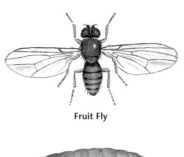

Fruit Fly

Grasshopper Nymph

Waxworm

Mealworm

Black Field Cricket

Insects make up the bulk of most lizard diets and are full of protein.

(Illustrations not drawn to scale)

Fruit Flies *(Drosophila species)* These tiny flies are readily eaten by baby lizards.

Waxworms *(Galleria species)* These are a real treat but should not be used too often as they are very rich. They are good for taming your pet, or building up a weak or stressed individual. Feed waxworms by hand to prevent them wriggling away into the corners of the vivarium.

Mealworms *(Tenebrio species, Zoophobas species)* Some lizards find them difficult to digest, so observe your lizards when you first feed mealworms.

Crickets *(Gryllus species)* These are the most popular lizard food, ranging in size from pinhead to adult.

Beetle grubs Beetle larvae are big, fat, and very juicy, and suitable for all medium to large lizards.

Grasshoppers *(Locusta migratoria, Schistocerca gregaria)* These larger, fat-bodied insects are suitable for medium and large lizards, but you'll have to collect them yourself. They are able to climb, so they are more suitable for arboreal species, such as chameleons, rather than terrestrial ones like Leopard Geckos.

It is essential that you monitor how much your lizards eat to make sure that they are obtaining enough food. It may be easier to monitor the number of insects your lizard eats by feeding it in a separate container to the one in which it usually lives. Plastic pet homes are particularly suitable for this purpose.

We used to think that monitor lizards were carnivores. Now we know they are essentially insectivorous but they will enjoy and benefit from an occasional rodent in their diet. The mouse (*Mus musculus*) is the most readily available rodent food. It should be stored frozen and then thoroughly defrosted for about 1 hour at room temperature before serving. If you breed your own rodents, they must be kept and then killed in a humane way.

Adult Savannah Monitors can consume several mice per sitting. Omnivores, such as chameleons and Bearded Dragons, also benefit from the occasional small mouse or pinky (hairless, juvenile mouse). Remember, it is important to remove uneaten foods.

OMNIVORES

Omnivores eat plant and animal matter. The omnivores covered in this book – Bearded Dragon, Blue-tongued Skink, and Veiled Chameleon – will be satisfied with a combination of the foods listed under the other three categories. Always make sure that foods are finely chopped to allow for ease of eating and that stale foods are removed the day following.

SUPPLEMENTS

A range of vitamins are now available for lizards. The most important ones contain minerals as well. Extra vitamins and minerals are added by dusting food insects with supplement powders. Some new products even claim to assist lizards in assimilating UVA and UVB lighting. The best option is to use all these products in moderation and at the correct dose.

Adult mouse

Pinkies

Leopard Gecko

Eublepharis macularius

Desert/terrestrial

Insectivore

20 years

8-9 in
(20-22 cm)

Leopard Geckos are one of the easiest lizards to keep as pets. They are clean, attractive, and, if cared for properly, they are unlikely to become ill or need veterinary treatment.

Spotted like the big cats that share their name, Leopard Geckos are adapted to life in the harsh, arid, rocky deserts of northwest India and Pakistan. These nocturnal lizards live alone or in small groups and avoid fatally hot daytime temperatures by hiding under rocks and boulders, emerging during the cooler night to seek out insect prey.

Leopard Geckos are in the family Eublepharidae. They have eyelids and lack adhesive toepads. They are a terrestrial (ground living) species. They also can vocalize, making soft clicking sounds at night.

Ideally, your Leopard Gecko should be housed on its own, where there is no competition for food or shelter. A 24 x 12 x 15 in (60 x 30 x 38 cm) vivarium provides ample space for a single specimen. However, if you do want to keep several lizards together, use a larger vivarium measuring approximately 36 x 12 x 15 in (90 x 30 x 38 cm). This would be suitable for a trio – all females, or two females and one male.

Having a larger vivarium will also give you an opportunity to make an attractive desert-style setup for your pets. Play sand, pea gravel, and wood chips can be used as a base or substrate. Live succulents and other house plants can also be added – simply bury a pot in the substrate and water your plants on a regular basis.

SIMILAR SPECIES

African Fat-tailed Gecko
Hemitheconyx caudicinctus

Providing a temperature range of 80-90°F (27-32°C) is maintained and your setup offers the essentials – food, water, and shelter – your gecko should be happy. Leopard Geckos are nocturnal and, although they are active at other times too in captivity, they do not need overhead lighting for heat. A nighttime drop in temperature to 70°F (21°C) is fine. A heat pad is the only requirement to make sure that your pet keeps warm. By placing it at one end of the vivarium your gecko

A plump tail is a sign of a healthy, well-fed Leopard Gecko.

The velvety skin texture feels soft to the touch.

Large eyes help to funnel available light.

Each toe has a tiny, almost invisible claw.

Gentle and calm, this small and attractive lizard makes an ideal introduction to keeping pet reptiles.

Leopard Geckos are quite variable in coloration. Some have much brighter yellow skin patches, while others have spots that form different shapes and patterns.

can warm up or cool down (thermoregulate) as it wishes.

Most reptiles will benefit from access to a humidity chamber within their vivarium. A box containing some plastic plants that are regularly mist sprayed is ideal. It is used to prevent dehydration and helps to encourage regular skin shedding.

Geckos are very clean and will select and use a chosen toilet site. Their dry droppings should be removed on a regular basis. Even if a

Once safely held, a tame Leopard Gecko will sit contentedly in your hands for quite a long period of time.

Observation Point

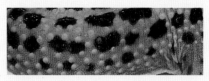

Skin

A Leopard Gecko sheds, or sloughs, its skin on a regular basis. The peeling skin is fine and translucent, and it is shed more frequently when a gecko is young. These lizards normally eat the skin because it is likely to be quite nutritious.

Look carefully at your lizard and notice how it fades in color as the process of shedding begins. A new, more colorful, layer is revealed underneath as they pick off the old skin or rub themselves against objects to aid peeling.

Keep a note of how often, and at what time of day or night, your gecko sheds its skin. Should you find a piece, hold it up to the light and you will see the exact pattern of your lizard's skin. Measure, or weigh, your gecko each time it sheds to give you a good idea of how much it grows during each stage of development.

number of geckos are kept together, most vivaria will require a thorough cleaning only once every few months.

Your pet should be offered food every day or so. However, a well-fed (plump-tailed) gecko can survive without any food for at least a week. They eat most small to medium-sized live foods, such as crickets and grasshoppers. You should leave a few insects in the vivarium for your lizard to stalk as desired. A young adult will eat about 5-6 insects at a sitting, several times a week.

Water should be kept in a shallow dish at ground level and replaced on a regular basis. Spraying the vivarium with water helps to create a humid microclimate for your pet and is also recommended.

Leopard Geckos are one of the easiest lizards to handle well. It is best to sit down when handling any reptile just in case it is dropped or jumps out of your hand. The best time to start taming your gecko is when it is still quite young. Handle for short, regular periods to show your pet that you will not harm it and, as its confidence grows, it should become even easier to handle.

Green Anole

Anolis carolinensis

Tropical/arboreal

Insectivore

3-5 years

5-8 in
(13-20 cm)

Anoles are small and charming lizards. Colorful and active, they leap and dart about providing hours of visual entertainment. Males possess a bright orange dewlap, an extendible flap of skin on the throat.

Native to the southern United States, Green Anoles can be found on walls, fences, and shrubs in gardens and other man-made settlements. They are active during daylight hours. Males are noted for their head bobbing displays, signalling each other with bright flashes of color from their throat fans.

Approximately 300 species and subspecies of anole are recognized and all have similar needs when kept in captivity.

Anoles will thrive in tall, tropical setups containing either real or artificial plants and branches.

Several may be kept together but, since males are highly territorial, a harem of four females to one male is about the best ratio for a

An anole's head is typically long – it is able to catch and consume its food easily.

This adult male shows the scars of territorial battles. Males are also brighter and larger than females.

community setup. The most suitable vivarium would measure at least 36 x 24 x 12 in (90 x 60 x 30 cm). To minimize competition for the "best" basking spot, offer two or more basking areas and numerous retreats, usually created by the plants you provide. A full-spectrum

fluorescent light will assist in the healthy development of lizards and plants. A daytime temperature range of 74-86°F (23-30°C) should be maintained. At night temperatures can safely drop to 68°F (20°C).

These insectivores will eat any small to medium live insect foods: make sure they have a wide variety. Feed at least twice weekly by releasing several live insects into the vivarium, watching to ensure that every occupant obtains at least two insects per feeding. A small surplus amount of live food may be present in the vivarium at all times. By observing your anoles you will soon learn to judge whether they are actually hungry rather than just greedy for another plump cricket.

Mist spraying once a day or so is essential because anoles love humidity and prefer to drink water droplets from leaves rather than from a bowl. Generally, they do not handle well, but your anole will soon learn to jump down onto your hand for a tasty treat, such as a waxmoth larva. By keeping still and calm, your anole will be less nervous of you and your movements.

Here the skin color is green but it can change to brown very quickly.

Tails are often damaged, but they often regrow into a stub like this one.

Long, fine fingers, toepads, and claws enable anoles to grip and climb very quickly.

Anoles are very agile, active lizards. They run fast, delighting the observer as they leap about. Males display with their colorful throat fans.

SIMILAR SPECIES

Brown Anole
Anolis sagrei

Uromastyx

Uromastyx acanthinurus

Desert/terrestrial

Herbivore

7-15 years

18 in
(45 cm)

These tough-looking lizards thrive in the harsh desert-like conditions found in the southern Mediterranean and Middle East. Uromastyx have a dry, parchment-like skin on their large, chunky frame. Skin color varies widely from dull brown to yellow or brick red. They are quite inquisitive and make endearing pets, with their tortoise-like head and postures. In captivity, they are friendly and unlikely to hurt the careful keeper.

All Uromastyx are best kept individually because they are not a social species. Juveniles are reared best in small plastic pet-home-type units. Larger individuals and adults require vivaria large enough to run about in – a vivarium measuring 48 x 20 x 20 in (120 x 50 x 50 cm) is adequate for one lizard.

Gravel or sand, together with some sturdy rocks, make an excellent vivarium base and it is best to provide a few retreats at the cooler end. In the wild, basking rocks can reach 120°F, so

SIMILAR SPECIES

Rock Agama
Laudakia stellio

to avoid overheating a Uromastyx will retreat into cool burrows. These are easily made from drainpipe or cork logs. However, do ensure that no heavy rocks or logs are positioned carelessly, since they could collapse and injure your pet, which is quite inquisitive and will soon investigate any changes within their vivarium.

Offer water a couple of times a week in shallow accessible dishes. Mist spray occasionally and a monthly bath, or soak, in a large dish is likely to be appreciated.

It is important to give these lizards the benefit of both full-spectrum fluorescent lights and the heat output of a ceramic heater, safely controlled by a thermostat. At the hottest point in the vivarium temperatures should reach 100°F (38°C). The other areas need to be considerably cooler at 68-72°F (20-22°C). This temperature gradient is much easier to achieve in larger vivaria. During the night the heat can drop to about 65°F (18°C).

The Uromastyx is almost totally herbivorous and its diet should consist of mainly green leaf foods with pieces of vegetable and fruit added. Tougher food items need to be chopped up, especially for juveniles, which have weaker jaws. Carrots, peas, beans, and hibiscus leaves are also enjoyed. The Uromastyx is also called the Date Palm Lizard in some areas, so it is worth providing fresh dates if available. Some insect foods may be accepted, but should only form up to 3% of the diet. Feed your pet every other day.

Do not worry unduly if your Uromastyx rests without eating for 1-2 weeks in one of its favorite retreats. In the wild, this species estivates, that is, it spends the summer or dry conditions in a dormant state, at least for short periods.

Uromastyx are not nervous creatures and if you are patient, especially if you are starting out with a juvenile, your lizard will come to you for food. Slow movements are less likely to startle your pet and eventually it should sit on your hand, at least for a while. Like other medium-sized lizards you can pick them up gently with one or two hands.

A small and plump captive-bred juvenile is the best choice because it will easily adapt to life in the vivarium.

Tough and chunky inhabitants of hostile desert environments, Uromastyx still enjoy an occasional bath or spray with tepid water.

A wide mouth helps the Uromastyx to graze and tear at vegetation.

The armoured spiky scales on the tail act as a formidable weapon.

Peacock Day Gecko

Phelsuma quadriocellata

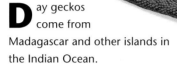
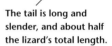

Tropical/arboreal

Insectivore

10 years

3 in
(7.5 cm)

Day geckos come from Madagascar and other islands in the Indian Ocean.

The Peacock Day Gecko is a delightful little jewel and can make a vivarium come alive with flashes of color as it patrols its territory. It gets its name from the peacock-like eye marking on each side of the body just behind the front legs. A combination of red spots and blobs on its back and an overall turquoise skin color makes this a very striking little lizard. Compared to other day geckos, this spotted variety is a dwarf species reaching only 3 in (7.5 cm) in length.

A vivarium measuring 20 x 12 x 24 in (50 x 30 x 60 cm) is only suitable for one male or a pair. With larger vivaria it is much easier to create a suitable environment for both you and your lizards to enjoy – it is like having your own natural history television program "live" in your home.

The tail is long and slender, and about half the lizard's total length.

I have a 40 x 36 x 18 in (100 x 90 x 45 cm) glass vivarium for my day geckos. It has enough space for fluorescent tubes that are hidden above a mesh screen, which helps to provide fresh air. The temperature range is maintained at 77-90°F (25-32°C). As night falls a timer switches off the spotlight and the temperature falls to a cooler 68-72°F (20-22°C). Mist spraying every morning and evening should keep

SIMILAR SPECIES

Gold-dust Day Gecko
Phelsuma laticauda

These are some of the most beautifully colored lizards in the world.

These geckos will display to each other with tail wagging and head bobbing movements.

A long tongue helps this diurnal lizard to lick and clean its eyes.

Because their skin tears very easily, day geckos are virtually impossible to hold. Enjoy them for what they are – lovely little creatures that leap about from leaf to leaf around their vivarium.

humidity levels high in glass vivaria.

Vivaria of this size are excellent for housing a harem, and under the right conditions you will find it difficult to stop them from breeding.

It is essential to keep only one male to a cage because the males are very territorial and will not tolerate any newcomers to an established group. Without adequate space, food, or basking opportunities, bullied individuals are less likely to survive in the vivarium. Their color soon fades and this is a sign that they are under stress or suffering from ill health. Such individuals must be rehoused separately.

A well-balanced planted vivarium can look wonderful, especially when your geckos are leaping from leaf to leaf. Broad-leaved plants, such as mother-in-law's tongue, *Sanservia* species, and philodendrons, *Philodendron* species, are effective. Bamboo poles create attractive decor and make great basking areas as long as they are placed safely away from, but in reach of, a bulb's rays. Ground substrate is not needed, but you can use lizard grass astroturf, or leaf litter and wood chips.

Day geckos are arboreal lizards and climbing or flying foods are relished. These small lizards should only be fed small foods, such as small crickets and waxmoth larvae, dusted with recommended amounts of vitamin and mineral supplements. Their habit of licking nectar is well known and a mixture of equal parts of honey, peach or pear baby food, and water is readily eaten.

Standing's Day Gecko

Phelsuma standingi

Tropical/arboreal

Insectivore

10 years

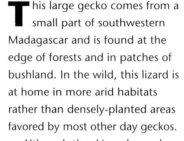

10 in
(25 cm)

This large gecko comes from a small part of southwestern Madagascar and is found at the edge of forests and in patches of bushland. In the wild, this lizard is at home in more arid habitats rather than densely-planted areas favored by most other day geckos.

Although the skin color and patterns vary in this species, they tend to have sky-blue skin with a green head and black, net-like, crazy paving patterns.

Like all day geckos, these lizards spend very little time on the ground. Some keepers prefer to line the vivarium with newspaper, but you can use large pebbles or other natural decor. Establish growing plants within the vivarium – mother-in-law's tongue, *Sanservia* species, and other hardy house plants are worth trying.

A pair or trio – 1 male and 2 females – can be housed spaciously in a 24 x 24 x 24 in (60 x 60 x 60 cm) vivarium. Mist spraying is required for drinking. In comparison to other day geckos, this species seems to prefer slightly higher, more steady temperatures

This is one of the largest, most attractive, and frequently bred of all day geckos.

Although small, the ear opening is clearly visible in all day geckos.

of about 90°F (32°C) and lower humidity levels of 70-75%. At night, as temperatures drop to 65-72°F (18-22°C), they will sleep on leaves or in a sheltered piece of bark.

These geckos are more tolerant of their young than other day geckos. A British breeder, Simon King, reports that juveniles

hatching out of eggs in the same vivarium as breeding pairs are able to live as a family. However, the young males should be removed as soon as they mature.

Large day geckos can eat most insects currently available to the enthusiast. Many home and garden caught invertebrates can also be offered but make sure they are from an organic rather than pesticide-sprayed part of your own environment. Beetle grubs and crickets are relished and most foodstuffs should be regularly dusted with vitamin and mineral supplements to ensure your pet lizard stays healthy. They really enjoy the honey-fruit mixture (page 29) and nectar – these should be placed high up in the vivarium in tiny bottle tops or upturned jam jar lids.

Insect food such as wax or mealworms can be placed in suspended plastic boxes that the lizard can reach when it is hungry, but from which the insects cannot escape. These insects will need pieces of fruit to make sure that they can eat and drink too.

To provide water, mist spray the vivarium. This gecko may learn to drink from a shallow dish if it is placed high up rather than on the ground.

Day geckos' skin will tear if you handle them so it is best to just observe them as they leap about in the vivarium.

Day gecko's actively hunt using sight to locate their prey.

Males usually have a broader based tail to encompass twinned reproductive organs.

Geckos are agile predators and are fast and acrobatic lizards.

Giant Day Gecko

Phelsuma madagascarensis

Tropical/arboreal

Insectivore

10 years

10 in
(25 cm)

These attractive, plump lizards are active and easy to keep and breed within the vivarium. Their skin is an electric lime green and they can have, depending on the exact subspecies, orangey-red markings in the form of dots or blobs along the back and particularly between the nostrils and eyes.

They are frequently found on palm trees in damp forests and within buildings on Madagascar and its surrounding islands. This type of habitat allows geckos plenty of surfaces on which to search for insects and a good opportunity to establish and retain a territory. Active by day, this large gecko can grow to 10 in (25 cm) in length, of which 6 in (15 cm) is its thick tubular tail.

These are agile lizards, leaping from leaf to leaf, and quickly scurrying into protective holes or beneath bark when threatened. Like many geckos they are adapted to an arboreal lifestyle. The

Day geckos can lose their tails in combat; however, usually they will regrow.

The enlarged toe pads give day geckos a strong grip.

SIMILAR SPECIES

House Gecko
Hemidactylus frenatus

•

Giant House Gecko
Hemidactylus mabouia

adhesive pads on each digit make sure that they get a good grip on shiny slippery leaves – and even glass or the sides of a vivarium – as well as the rough bark on trees and palms.

This is achieved because the underside of each toe is covered with extremely fine hair-like structures called setae, which enable these lizards to grip or cling to almost any surface. Many geckos can run across, and even live on, the ceiling of a room, feeding on insects that have been attracted by the light.

These round-bodied lizards are simple to care for and look terrific as their skin is electric lime green with bright markings.

A planted vivarium will make the most attractive display for these pretty geckos. A range of house plants may be selected from garden centers, but among the easiest to maintain within the vivarium are philodendrons, ficus, yuccas, orchids, hoya, ferns, citrus, oleander, and passion flower. The use of full-spectrum lamps will help both your plants and lizards to grow and develop naturally.

Some pruning will be required to keep your plants from over-running the vivarium. You must also make sure that growing plants do not interfere with heating or lighting equipment, or grow to such a density that they stop your geckos moving about their habitat.

Well rounded, muscular and plump, this lizard looks in excellent health.

The large eyes are kept clean by regular licks from the gecko's tongue.

Replicate a daytime tropical temperature range of 77-90°F (25-32° C) using small spotlights and heating pads. At night temperatures can drop to 68-72°F (20-22°C). These lizards enjoy humidity levels reaching 80%, so mist spray or add a bubbler bowl. Care must be taken within the vivarium to make sure that the environment does not become stale or moldy. These lizards really do appreciate fresh air, so make sure you keep your vivarium well ventilated.

Life in the wild is fraught with danger and day geckos have many predators, including birds, snakes, and other large lizards. Even without added dangers, their time is spent hunting for food and attempting, if male, to establish and hold a territory while avoiding any violent confrontations with other males.

These territorial disputes can result in mortal wounds, with bites easily ripping their delicate skin. It is best, therefore, to keep Giant Day Geckos singly or in a harem of one male to two females if space is available. A 24 x 18 x 12 in (60 x 45 x 30 cm) vivarium is fine for a solitary individual and a 24 x 24 x 24 in (60 x 60 x 60 cm) one is ample for 2-3 individuals.

If kept in adult groups, breeding is likely and it is very rewarding when the conditions within your own vivarium are such that your pets start to exhibit breeding behavior. Look out for the typical clutch of two hard shelled eggs of 0.4 in (1 cm) in diameter. These are usually wedged into a piece of wood or stuck to the sides of the vivarium.

The majority of foods eaten by these lizards is insect matter, and both crawling

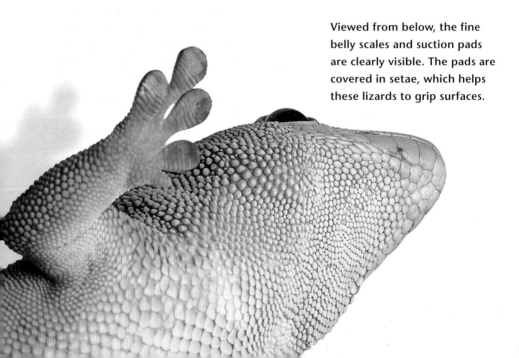

Viewed from below, the fine belly scales and suction pads are clearly visible. The pads are covered in setae, which helps these lizards to grip surfaces.

and flying insects are eaten with gusto. The Giant Day Gecko will eagerly lap sweet fruits and plant sap. A halved grape positioned securely, high in the vivarium, will attract a gecko. Almost any fruit may be offered. Honey-fruit mixture (p. 29) should be the dietary staple. Be sure to add essential minerals and vitamins to the diets of these lizards.

They love to drink water in droplet form, so spray your vivarium regularly to ensure they do not get thirsty. A water feature would also be suitable.

Giant Day Geckos are not the easiest lizards to handle. If physically restrained, you risk tearing their delicate skin and they are far too active to sit still in your hands or on you lap for very long. These lizards are, therefore, best left in the vivarium and enjoyed visually.

Observation Point

Fruity

Lizards, like people, can be quite individual in their food preferences. One may adore and only lick honey, while another will prefer grapes and mango baby food. Although most of their diet is made up of insects, the day gecko's sweet tooth gives you the opportunity to observe and cater to their particular tastes.

Test your lizard's preferences for different types of fruit and baby food fruit by placing measured amounts in small dishes around the vivarium. You can record how often and for how long they lick each item.

Inland Bearded Dragon

Pogona vitticeps

Desert/arboreal

Omnivore

7-12 years

16-24 in
(40-60 cm)

In the wild, these remarkable Australian natives are equally at home in lush suburban backyards or the more open and very hot desert scrubland. In captivity, they are noted for their ease of care and good temperament.

Bearded Dragons are medium-sized lizards, although they do tend to have heavy bodies. Their name is taken from their extendible black beard, which forms in mature males. The back, head, and tail are rough to the touch, while their belly is white and soft. A line of fine long spines runs along both sides of the body, which helps to camouflage the lizards by breaking up their visible outline when they press against a tree stump.

Unless you intend to breed these lizards, it is best to house and keep them alone, or to keep only females together. A vivarium measuring 30 x 20 x 30 in (76 x 51 x 76 cm) is fine for an adult pair or trio (1 male and 2 females).

SIMILAR SPECIES

Rankin's Dragon
Pogona brevis

You can buy juveniles when they are a couple of months old – they usually measure about 6-7 in (15-17 cm). Two young Beardies would need at least a 24 x 12 x 12 in (60 x 30 x 30 cm) vivarium for the first few months of their life.

These lizards require a dry woodland or desert-style vivarium. Provide cork logs or rocks for climbing on or burrowing under and cover the base with sand or bark chips. If two or more lizards are kept together, you need to provide several basking areas to reduce competition. Temperatures should reach about 104°F (40°C) at the hottest end of their setup to allow for basking and the cooler end should reach about 82°F (28°C).

At night the temperature needs to reduce right down to 68°F (20°C). Heating pads are useful to ensure the substrate is warm and dry at all times, and full-spectrum fluorescent lighting is essential for healthy growth and development. This diurnal species requires twelve hours of daylight, and a dark rest period is essential for sleep.

Your Bearded Dragon will enjoy the occasional mist spraying, and a clean shallow water dish should be available for drinking at all times. The water should be changed frequently and the soiled areas need regular cleaning.

These lizards are omnivorous and have a very good appetite. A diet supplemented with vitamins and minerals is recommended, especially for the faster growing juveniles. They respond to the movement of prey and will dash down from a basking spot to chase after any active insects they may spot – their favorites tend to be spiders and crickets. You can cool your bugs in the refrigerator to make them less active and easier for your pet to catch. A large range of foods may be

Often living in family groups, Bearded Dragons communicate with leg and tail movements, as well as head bobbing.

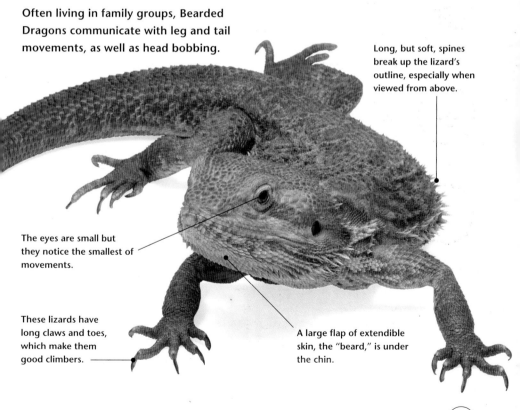

Long, but soft, spines break up the lizard's outline, especially when viewed from above.

The eyes are small but they notice the smallest of movements.

These lizards have long claws and toes, which make them good climbers.

A large flap of extendible skin, the "beard," is under the chin.

offered, including commercially raised insects, some processed dried lizard foods and an occasional pink mouse (for their nutritional value). Plant materials, such as mixed vegetables and dandelion leaves and flowers, are enjoyed and should be chopped for smaller individuals to manage easily. Feed your pet 4-5 times per week and do not forget to remove the feeding bowl and any old food the morning after feeding to prevent the food from turning bad.

A well-defined social hierarchy, or pecking order, develops within any group of Bearded Dragons and it is interesting to watch their behavior at feeding time. The largest or most dominant lizard will feed first, while the others wait and watch with their tails clearly bent upwards, signalling their lowly status.

Only after the dominant lizard has finished eating and moves away do the other subordinate lizards get their chance to feed. If keeping a group of Beardies, it is essential to provide enough basking sites and food so that all the members of your family group can thrive.

These lizards tame very quickly while they are still young and they are unlikely to try to bite you. Regular handling at this stage should ensure your lizard remains willing to be handled. If, however, your lizard is unwilling to be picked up, it will just walk or jump away.

Bearded Dragons make surprisingly friendly pets. This juvenile is getting to know the hand that feeds it.

Observation Point

Is mine a boy or girl lizard?

Lizards, just like a lot of animals and people, have visible characteristics that make it quite easy to identify the difference between a male and a female. Most lizards in this book can be easily sexed by the time they are about 1 year of age. It often helps to have several individuals of the same age placed together to be able to notice the differences and to correctly identify the sexes.

The following guide should help you to determine the most useful things to look out for when examining a lizard. If you need more professional help, ask a herpetologist (reptile and amphibian expert) or take your lizard, or photographs of it, to a meeting of your local herpetological society.

Body size

Most, but not, all male lizards are larger and stronger looking than their female counterparts.

Tail length

Males usually have thicker and longer tails than females. For example, male Blue-tongued Skinks have chunkier tails than the females.

Head variations

Males have larger, more colorful dewlaps and bigger head crests than females. Some males even have horns.

Anal and thigh pores

Females either lack or have much less prominent pores around the thighs and bottom area. To examine these you need to hold a lizard firmly and turn it upside down. The pores look just like ordinary scales but are often marked with a dimple and clearly visible as a "V" shape just beside the anal opening.

FEMALE

MALE

Blue-Tongued Skink

Tiliqua scincoides

Tropical/terrestrial

Omnivore

10 years

20 in
(50 cm)

There are at least a thousand known types of skink and they all have certain characteristics in common. They are noted for their long flattened bodies and reduced limbs – some have very small and very weak legs, while others are completely limbless.

However, few skinks are as attractive or easy to keep or breed as the magnificent blue-tongued species. These stocky lizards have overlapping scales and can be found in Australia and Tasmania where they live at ground level in leaf litter, eating invertebrates, snails, and fruit.

As their name suggests, these lizards have a big blue tongue. If threatened, this can be flattened and rippled inside an open mouth which, accompanied by a hiss, acts as an effective deterrent. This species, like most skinks, gives birth to live young, rather than laying eggs. Skinks are crepuscular, which means that they are active during the day, but particularly at dawn and dusk.

A long, cylindrical body helps this lizard burrow into leaf debris searching for food.

The large, wide, wedge-shaped mouth is ideal for crunching shells.

A dry, woodland type of habitat is ideal for this terrestrial species. The ground can be covered in cork logs for retreats and decorated with leaf litter, twigs, and mossy rocks. These lizards root around under ground debris looking for food, so you do not need a delicately planted vivarium.

A vivarium for a single skink should measure at least 48 x 12 x 12 in (120 x 30 x 30 cm). The combination of a heating pad and a thermostatically controlled spotlight, wired up to a timer switch, at one end will warm the tank and create a daytime basking area. Timing the light to

SIMILAR SPECIES

Pink-tongued Skink
Hemisphaerodon gerrardi

switch off during the evening will reduce the temperature. The daytime temperature gradient should be 77-95°F (25-35°C), falling to 65-68°F (18-20°C) at night.

To feed your pet place food in shallow dishes and feed fresh food daily or every other day. These scavenging omnivores enjoy dog/cat food with fruit – ripe banana and soft sweet fruits such as mango.

My own Blue-tongued Skink, Sydney, is fond of garden snails (*Helix aspersa*). These are scattered around the vivarium to encourage foraging. He crushes and spits out the shell before swallowing the soft snail. Garden snails may be collected and maintained in plastic pet homes for use over the winter period.

Water should be available to drink at all times and these lizards also love a mist spray. The moist conditions stimulate the skink to emerge and look for food.

They are normally very tolerant of handling and will tolerate the occasional stroke or scratch. Just as you would when handling other animals, remember to wash your hands after touching them.

Female skinks have more slender tails than males.

Banded patterns provide excellent camouflage on the ground.

Naturally very tolerant of handling, Blue-tongued Skinks are considered a good pet for close contact.

Savannah Monitor

Varanus exanthematicus

Tropical/terrestrial

Carnivore

10-15 years

40 in
(100 cm)

Savannah Monitors are found in North African countries such as Ghana, Togo, and Kenya.

The Savannah, or Bosc, Monitor is a species well suited to the hobbyist. Its remarkable character means that these square-jawed lizards can become extremely tame and placid. In fact, they can be so relaxed as to have a tendency to slothfulness and obesity if overfed and underexercised.

These lizards are solitary creatures and should be housed individually, only bringing adults together if breeding is desired. A vivarium measuring 48 x 18 x 18 in (120 x 45 x 45 cm) should be adequate for one baby. Adults need a vivarium at least 72 x 36 x 36 in. These lizards require the most sturdy furnishings – rocks, logs, and heavy-duty water bowls.

A shelter of cork or drainpipe is essential towards the cooler end of the vivarium. Some moveable furnishings are useful since they can be positioned safely and will offer temporary refuge for insects. This will encourage natural foraging activity as your monitor moves the pebbles with its snout or leg to obtain the tasty bugs. Smaller stones or wood chips are of no use since they would be thrown out of the way.

A simple setup is recommended, using newspaper as a floor covering or substrate with just a couple of main objects for basking on and hiding within.

A temperature gradient should be established. A suitable daytime range would be 83-90°F (28-32°C) at the hottest point, falling to 65°F (24°C) at night when the lizard sleeps. This lizard is crepuscular, which means it is particularly active at the beginning and end of each day, when temperatures are warming or cooling.

SIMILAR SPECIES

Black-Throated Rock Monitor
Varanus albogularis

Mist spraying twice-weekly should keep the humidity up to the required level of about 60%. Bathing is much enjoyed by monitors and a weekly soak is sufficient to ensure your lizard gets enough moisture and provides the option of a long drink.

Many lizards defecate in their water bowls, so the bowls must be regularly cleaned and fresh water given whenever fouling is noticed.

Monitors catch and consume their food whole and they really do seem to "smile" after swallowing a particularly tasty item. Offer your monitor larger insects and an occasional pink mouse. Adults will eat larger insects and whole adult mice. Feed as much as will be eaten in a 3-5 minute period, 2-3 times a week. Monitors are lazy if food is easy to get, so do encourage exercise. Live insects scattered in the vivarium will encourage foraging. At any age monitors also enjoy eating eggs. Serve one raw mixed up with a few grasshoppers or the commercial canned diet. It is a messy but enjoyable treat. Chicken is also enjoyed but, because most raw chicken has the potential to be contaminated with salmonella, it should be cooked before feeding.

If purchased young, Savannah Monitors should become very tame and are suited to occasional handling. Temperaments vary but, on the whole, these monitors are placid, thrive in captivity, and tolerate handling. I have had many years' experience handling these lizards and I have never had any problems with aggression. However, if one should bite you, it would be similar to that of a dog or cat bite – painful and probably requiring medical attention.

The long neck is useful for reaching into holes and burrows.

Monitor lizards have heavy "armored" scales and long sharp claws for digging and climbing.

These lizards are easy to keep and their placid nature has endeared the Savannah Monitor to reptile keepers around the world.

Plumed Basilisk

Basiliscus plumifrons

Tropical/arboreal

Insectivore

10 years

29 in
(72 cm)

Few lizards are as magnificently adorned as the Plumed Basilisk, with its yellow eyes and bright green crests. The males are larger and more impressive looking than the females, and are adorned with a large crest on the head, along the back (dorsal crest), and on the tail. These are vibrant green and they are often marked with rows of blue spots. These lizards are the athletic sprinters of the jungle, able to run at speeds of 18 mph (29 km/h) over short distances.

This young Plumed Basilisk is a popular species. Captive-bred stocks are available.

Recently hatched, this juvenile lacks the fine crest and colors of an adult.

Long feet help this lizard to run quickly.

Plumed Basilisks inhabit a small area of tropical Central America. They are found only in Costa Rica, Panama, and Nicaragua, where you may catch a glimpse of one sunning itself on a tree trunk in a jungle clearing. They can take flight in an instant, and they have the ability to run across open stretches of water, earning themselves the name of "Jesus" lizards among local peoples.

There are four species of basilisk, including the plumed species, and they all live in similar habitats – Common Basilisk (*Basiliscus basiliscus*), Red-headed Basilisk (*Basiliscus galeritus*), and the Central American Basilisk (*Basiliscus vittatus*). Only the common and plumed species are occasionally available from captive-bred stocks.

Plumed Basilisks require spacious accommodation. A juvenile needs a 36 x 12 x 18 in (90 x 30 x 45 cm) vivarium to begin with and then you will eventually have to make them a custom built unit that measures about 6.6 ft (2 m) in length and 5 ft (1.5 m) in height once they become adult. To thrive, males should always be housed individually or they will fight and harass one another. If space permits, several females may be kept together with a single male.

They enjoy daytime temperatures of about 75-86°F (24-30°C) with a bright basking area of 95°F. At night the temperature should fall to around 68-75°F (20-24°C), as it would in the wild. The humidity should be between 70-85%, so mist spray every other day.

A large water bowl is essential, and so is a lush, tropical background of real or plastic plants together with a sturdy branch by, or over, the water bowl. Other branches for climbing and basking on are appreciated, and your pet will climb to quite a height to catch some light rays or

Fantastic green camouflage helps this lizard to blend into the jungle scenery.

Nicknamed the Jesus lizard, this basilisk can run across water.

These lizards can become quite tame if handled regularly.

flying insects. Some shelter should be provided – cork logs are ideal as retreats.

In larger vivaria it is often possible to keep similar-sized iguanas and basilisks. together. Generally, they do not seem to mind the company of other larger lizards. However, snakes and lizards do not get on well and therefore should not be kept together.

Basilisks are fond of most of the available medium and large insects. They benefit from an occasional small rodent, especially when you want to make them ready for breeding. Adult rodents are too big, so keep to pinky or fuzzy mice.

Some plant material will also be eaten, and any of the foods considered suitable for omnivorous or herbivorous reptiles can be offered once or twice a week.

However, make sure they do not become overweight, especially as a result of their own greediness. Juveniles thrive on well-supplemented small insects, such as young crickets, waxmoth larvae, and beetle grubs, as well as a few leaves.

If handled regularly, basilisks can become quite tame, but they are generally kept because they are wonderful to look at and observe. Never handle one outside because you are likely to lose it – like many lizards, they have the amazing ability to sit as still as a stone one minute and then to take off at great speed in a flash with no warning. These lizards possess long nails, so they benefit from the occasional nail clip. Make sure the "quick" (living vein) running through each toe is not cut.

Observation Point

Feet

Look around your own natural environment and notice how the feet of different animals are adapted to suit their surroundings. The foot of a domestic cat, a nocturnal hunter, is very well adapted and has extremely sharp retractable claws for catching and tearing. Most birds, like their lizard relatives, have feet and claws for gripping.

The basilisk's foot is uniquely adapted to enable them to avoid predators. They have delicate, enlarged flaps of scaled skin along the digits of their hind feet. On the downward movement of the foot upon water these flaps open and, like a webbed foot, exert a greater resistance to the water. At great speed, and without sinking, these lizards can quite literally run on water to escape their predators. It is worth trying to get a closer look at this lizard's feet as it moves around the vivarium.

Other lizards have specially adapted feet too. The chameleon's foot looks almost painfully split, with three digits fused together one way and two the other (see page 54). This provides this arboreal lizard with the unique ability to grasp entirely any suitably-sized branches. Iguanas have a long fourth toe which, together with sharp claws, enable them to climb high into forest canopies (see page 59). Day geckos, as we have already seen, have amazing sticky pads, which possess fine hair-like structures to help them grip to sheer and smooth-looking surfaces.

Water Dragon

Physignathus concincinus

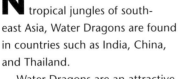

Tropical/arboreal

Carnivore

10-15 years

28-40 in
(70-100 cm)

Native to the tropical jungles of south-east Asia, Water Dragons are found in countries such as India, China, and Thailand.

Water Dragons are an attractive diurnal lizard. Their overall color is green, but the cheeks (jowls) of more mature males are enlarged, chubby, and adorned with large pink scales.

Larger vivaria suit these semi-arboreal lizards and a 36 x 36 x 36 in (90 x 90 x 90 cm) vivarium gives you room to incorporate the essential equipment for optimum care of your pet. Male Water Dragons are less aggressive to one another than other species, but I would recommend keeping males separately or in the company of one or more females only. For the first year of life, juveniles can be kept in smaller units measuring 36 x 12 x 18 in (90 x 30 x 45 cm).

These reptiles prefer semi-moist tropical conditions. An overall daytime temperature of about 77-82°F (25-28°C) should

The long tail helps this agile hunter to balance properly.

A row of erect, dragon-like scales run along the back.

Water Dragons love to bask on logs overhanging water.

A popular choice with pet keepers, Water Dragons are a very handleable larger lizard.

be maintained with a hotspot temperature of 92–96°F. A temperature range of 68-72°F (20-22°C) would be fine at night. A substrate of chunky wood chips, logs, and dense areas of real, or plastic, plants will help to create the right conditions for your pet.

It is worth ensuring that the light/heat source is protected so that you and your pet cannot burn. A full-spectrum fluorescent light is also very important to supply valuable ultra-violet light to these lizards, and to the real plants.

Long claws may need trimming in captivity.

Primarily insectivorous, Water Dragons will eat some vegetative matter, possibly up to 10% of their total diet.

Juveniles will feed mainly on small crickets, waxworms, and beetle grubs. As they grow, offer them an occasional pink mouse and, eventually, an adult mouse. Finely chopped fruits and watercress are likely to be tried by at least some young lizards.

Adults feed greedily and may consume large insects such as locusts and giant mealworms. Dandelion leaves and flowers, and even chopped pears or peaches, can be offered. Feed your young lizards every other day and then every 2-3 days as they mature. This amount of food should be sufficient without overfeeding.

Regularly supplement the diet as these lizards need calcium and vitamins, such as Vitamin D_3, to grow and remain healthy.

Mist spraying is enjoyed by these lizards and a large dish filled with water should always be available. They will bathe, drink from it, and may use it as a toilet, so regular cleaning is essential. However, the water soiling habit does eventually benefit the keeper because the substrate remains clean for long periods of time.

Water Dragons tame well, are easily bred, and are suitable for occasional handling. These lizards can be a bit unpredictable because they can remain static for long periods of time, but are then liable to run off when you least expect it.

Veiled Chameleon

Chamaeleo calyptratus

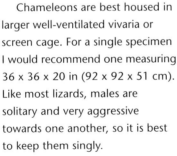

Desert/arboreal

Omnivore

2-8 years

24 in
(60 cm)

Also called the Yemen Chameleon, this lizard is native to Saudi Arabia and Yemen – hot, arid lands of the Middle East. They do, however, frequent lush pockets of vegetation such as oases and plantation areas.

Males are bigger than females and males also have a much larger head crest. This species is captive bred in large numbers and seems to be one of the most adaptable chameleon species for the pet keeper willing to invest some effort.

Chameleons are best housed in larger well-ventilated vivaria or screen cage. For a single specimen I would recommend one measuring 36 x 36 x 20 in (92 x 92 x 51 cm). Like most lizards, males are solitary and very aggressive towards one another, so it is best to keep them singly.

As bush or shrub dwellers, it is vital to provide your chameleon with living plants, or at least some sturdy plastic plants, and branches on which it can climb.

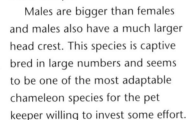
With one or more key "hot spots" your chameleon can warm up in the morning before spending the daylight hours periodically resting, basking, looking for prey, and avoiding predators!

A daytime temperature gradient of about 68-86°F (20-30°C) should be maintained, which may drop to 60°F (15°C) at night. Add a full-spectrum light tube to ensure good plant and pet growth.

Chameleons need to eat and drink regularly. Water is preferred in droplet form so mist spray daily. All live foods can be offered, but climbing or flying insects are preferred. Vary your chameleon's diet to provide a suitable range of vitamins and minerals for healthy development.
Larger Veiled

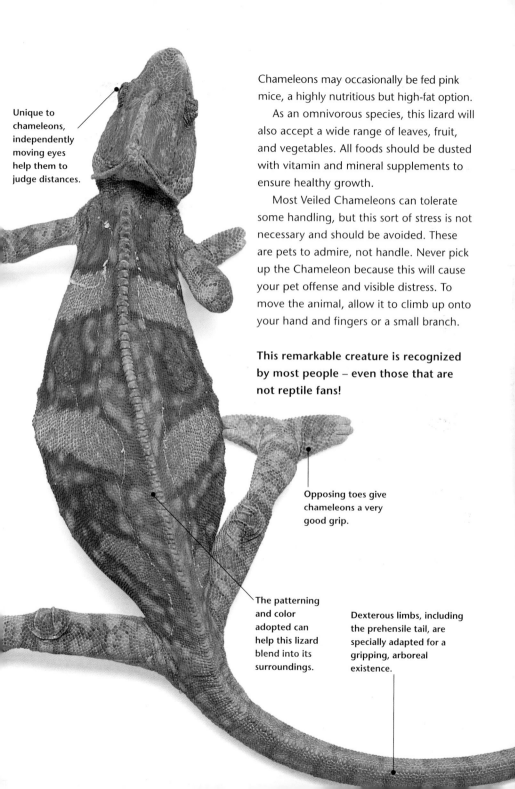

Unique to chameleons, independently moving eyes help them to judge distances.

Chameleons may occasionally be fed pink mice, a highly nutritious but high-fat option.

As an omnivorous species, this lizard will also accept a wide range of leaves, fruit, and vegetables. All foods should be dusted with vitamin and mineral supplements to ensure healthy growth.

Most Veiled Chameleons can tolerate some handling, but this sort of stress is not necessary and should be avoided. These are pets to admire, not handle. Never pick up the Chameleon because this will cause your pet offense and visible distress. To move the animal, allow it to climb up onto your hand and fingers or a small branch.

This remarkable creature is recognized by most people – even those that are not reptile fans!

Opposing toes give chameleons a very good grip.

The patterning and color adopted can help this lizard blend into its surroundings.

Dexterous limbs, including the prehensile tail, are specially adapted for a gripping, arboreal existence.

Panther Chameleon

Furcifer pardalis

Tropical/arboreal

Insectivore

2-5 years

20 in
(51 cm)

Chameleons are a wonder of the natural world and are noted for many unusual features – amazing color-changing abilities, independently moving eyes, and an incredible, extendible tongue.

Panther Chameleons are large and colorful lizards that are well worth the extra care required to ensure their survival within the vivarium. Native to Madagascar, the home of most chameleons, they can also be found on a few neighboring islands, such as Mauritus and Reunion. They have been deliberately introduced onto these islands to control insect pests on plantations.

Unless a large enclosure is available for a pair or trio (one male and two females), these chameleons are best kept singly. Males are very territorial and will fight and injure one another if kept together. If housed on their own, they appear to be easier to keep

The long tail is prehensile and acts like a fifth limb.

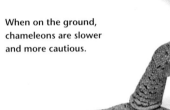

When on the ground, chameleons are slower and more cautious.

Male Panther Chameleons may be green, red, orange, lemon yellow, or even turquoise in color. Females are much less colorful and tend to have peachy orange patches.

and are less nervous than the females. Even seeing another chameleon in a vivarium that is in close proximity can upset some individuals.

I would recommend a well-ventilated vivarium of no less than 24 x 24 x 24 in (60 x 60 x 60 cm) for juveniles or solitary individuals. However, an optimum size for an enclosure would be 24 x 72 x 24 in (60 x 180 x 60 cm), the greater height providing more scope to create a more naturalistic setup.

Emotions, as well as camouflage, are partly responsible for the array of colors that are exhibited.

The mouth is large and the jaws are strong. This enables chameleons to catch and crunch quite large prey.

A daytime temperature gradient of 80-95°F (27-35°C) is ideal, while at night the temperature can drop to 72°F (22°C). A full-spectrum light tube is essential for healthy growth unless regular exposure to natural sunlight is available. This is difficult to achieve in cooler, temperate climates like the northern part of the United States. Do remember, however, never to place your vivarium near a window to provide extra sunshine for your pet. The useful ultraviolet rays will not penetrate glass or plastic and may turn your vivarium into an oven instead – the direct sunlight lifting the temperature to a fatally high level.

Add one or more spotlights to create a suitable basking area. Provide branches and plants, real or plastic, for your pet to climb on.

These chameleons prefer high humidity levels of about 75% for at least part of the day, and they also prefer to drink water from droplets on leaves. Compared to other lizards, they do tend to drink a lot of water and inhabit areas in the wild with high

P a n t h e r   C h a m e l e o n   (53)

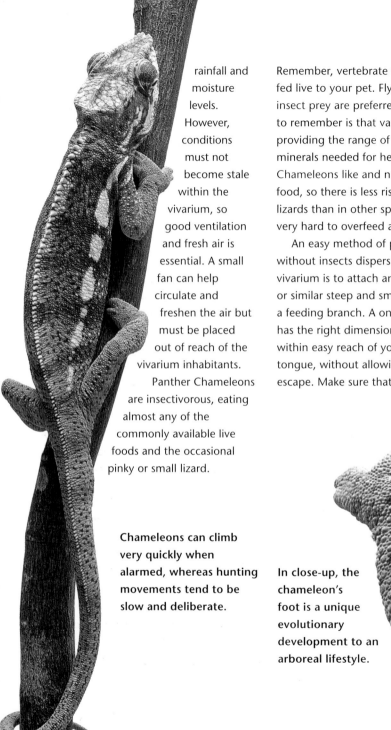

rainfall and moisture levels. However, conditions must not become stale within the vivarium, so good ventilation and fresh air is essential. A small fan can help circulate and freshen the air but must be placed out of reach of the vivarium inhabitants.

Panther Chameleons are insectivorous, eating almost any of the commonly available live foods and the occasional pinky or small lizard.

Remember, vertebrate food should not be fed live to your pet. Flying or climbing insect prey are preferred. The main thing to remember is that variety is the key to providing the range of vitamins and minerals needed for healthy development. Chameleons like and need quite a lot of food, so there is less risk of obesity in these lizards than in other species. It is actually very hard to overfeed a chameleon.

An easy method of providing live foods without insects dispersing into the vivarium is to attach an opaque pet home, or similar steep and smooth-sided bowl, to a feeding branch. A one-pound coffee can has the right dimensions. This will put food within easy reach of your pet and its tongue, without allowing the bugs to escape. Make sure that the bug home is

Chameleons can climb very quickly when alarmed, whereas hunting movements tend to be slow and deliberate.

In close-up, the chameleon's foot is a unique evolutionary development to an arboreal lifestyle.

well stocked and that the bugs are well fed – the chameleon will use this "service station" for a top up.

Chameleons drink a lot of water compared to other reptiles and prefer to drink it in droplet form rather than as still water in a bowl. Mist spray the vivarium daily and/or provide a pool with water circulating and dripping off branches back into the pool.

Chameleons are pets that are to be admired, not handled. Physical contact stresses them and is rarely necessary. Never pick up a chameleon as this will cause it great offense. If you need to move your chameleon to another cage, let it climb up onto your hand and fingers.

The skin contains many chromatophores – pigment-filled cells – which enable rapid change in skin coloration.

Green Iguana

Iguana iguana

Tropical/arboreal

Herbivore

10-15 years

6 ft
(1.8 m)

One of the most easily recognized and familiar reptiles in the world, iguanas are large tree-climbing lizards that graze on leaves, fruits, and flowers in lush tropical habitats.

These lizards are generally green, but a large variety of skin colors and patterns can be found in different populations and within the various subspecies of iguana. The family Iguanidae is good-sized and virtually all the members are found in the tropical Americas; they are also egg layers. Other species that belong to this family are the desert iguanas or "dipsos" (*Dipsosaurus* sp.), the chuck wallers, and the spiny-tailed iguanas.

Green Iguanas are natives of tropical Central and South America where they prefer living in the vicinity of lakes, rivers, or the sea. These diurnal dinosaurs bask in the sun on branches that overhang the water, sometimes at

A big lizard, the iguana is farmed for food in its native South America.

Dark patches on the flank and belly aid camouflage in shadowy vegetation.

quite considerable heights and, if disturbed, they drop into the water below. Iguanas are good climbers, swimmers, divers, and runners.

These magnificent creatures are suitable only for those pet keepers with the considerable space required to keep them and the ability to deal with the occasional aggression displayed by mature males.

Iguanas are large and impressive animals. They can become very tame but they require spacious accommodation for their long-term well being.

A long fourth finger and toe assist with gripping and climbing.

The muscular tail is an excellent tool for balance.

Iguanas need more space as they mature, height being the most important factor to consider. A juvenile would require a vivarium measuring at least 36 x 18 x 18 in (92 x 38 x 38 cm), whereas an adult requires a custom made unit measuring at least 48 x 72 x 48 in (120 x 180 x 120 cm). Increasingly, iguana owners use small rooms or walk-in vivaria incorporating sliding, double-glass doors available at home improvement stores. Iguanas should be kept individually.

For substrate, use wood chips, leaf litter, pebbles, or any similar material, including reptile grass, a type of astroturf, and newspaper. Sturdy branches for climbing and basking on and plastic plants for shade should be provided, together with a large non-spillable water bowl. No delicate plants are required for this active lizard, who would quickly destroy real plants. Cork logs make good retreats.

During the daytime a hot basking spot, 95°F, is needed, while temperatures at the cooler end of the vivarium should be approximately 77°F (25°C). At night the temperature can drop to 75°F (24°C). A full-spectrum, ultra-violet light tube is essential to maintain your lizard's health over the long term. Iguanas enjoy being mist sprayed immensely, but make sure the vivarium does not get too damp.

Observation Point

Defense

Lizards can defend themselves in a variety of ways. They may escape their predator by simply running away or, by keeping still and changing color, prevent a predator from seeing them. They may also hiss, parachute away, burrow, or swim. Some lizards pretend to be dead, some inflate their size, others have weapons to defend themselves, for example, with spiky tails. By using one or more of the above methods, most lizards live their lives and try to survive long enough to produce offspring of their own.

Iguanas defend themselves in various ways, with camouflage being their first line of defense. Their color helps them to blend in with their surroundings, and the jagged spines along the back are useful for breaking up their outline. If face-to-face with a predator, they can extend their dewlap and flatten the body to appear larger, and the long tail can act as an effective whip. In the wild, if they are still threatened, they can climb higher or jump from a branch into a river or the sea below.

The Plumed Basilisk also uses disguise, but if it remains under threat it has the remarkable ability to dash off across water into another bush, where it will again keep very still to avoid detection.

Many lizards use autonomy for defense; that is, when they are attacked the tail fractures, or breaks off, but keeps on wriggling. As the predator is diverted by this, the lizard has a chance to escape – in time, it will grow another tail. Some of the lizards in this book can drop their tails, but in general those chosen by pet keepers are species that do not do so.

Young herpetologists as well as zoos are still finding out more about how lizards defend themselves in the wild. The more you observe your iguana, the more you will learn and understand.

Adult iguanas are herbivorous and will eat a wide variety of foods. Fill a large bowl with a mixture of fruits, leaves, and vegetables and feed every other day or so. Remove the food bowl on the following day and replace with fresh food, at the latest, every third day.

Juvenile iguanas will eat much the same thing as the adults but in a smaller, more finely chopped form. They also will eat very limited amounts of live foods – cricket, grasshoppers, and waxworms. Taming and feeding your iguana goes hand in hand, and you need to invest

This Green Iguana is feeding hungrily on a fruit and vegetable salad. Remember to replenish your pet's feeding bowl regularly.

considerable time so that you can both enjoy a good relationship.

Provide your iguana with a large water bowl to drink from. They tend to defecate into this so make sure that it is changed

Scales cover every part of a lizard's body – including each and every toe, as seen on this iguana's foot.

and thoroughly cleaned every other day or so. They enjoy being mist sprayed, especially when shedding their skin.

Very tame iguanas may be walked on a lead or perched on a shoulder, but most of them never tame to this extent. Taking a large iguana out into public places can result in serious liability for the owner. Their claws can grow to quite a length and can lacerate human flesh, so trim them occasionally, taking care to avoid the "quick," or living part of the claw.

Less tame individuals need professional restraining – using long leather gauntlets to protect yourself is recommended. Hold the iguana firmly behind the neck and above the rear legs, tucking the tail under your arm to avoid its painful whip.

Record Card

All sorts of interesting information and measurements can be included on a record card. Begin by noting the size or weight of your pet when it is purchased. Record how often and what it feeds on, and keep a record of humidity levels, temperature, shedding, and your pet's activities.

Scientists and naturalists learn about animals by studying their behavior and by taking notes and measurements. So little is known about the behavior and lifestyles of many lizards that keeping records helps us to understand the animals we keep. It will help you to learn about the habits and preferences of your pet. You may like to photograph or sketch your pet. Almost every lizard has different markings, especially on the head, so you will be able to distinguish it from any others.

If your pet becomes ill, it may help you or your veterinarian to treat it more accurately if you have a record of its life history. It will also be a useful source of information if anyone has to look after your pet if you are ill or on vacation.

Here are some of the things you may wish to record:

- Common name and scientific name
- Date of birth (or purchase) and origin of pet
- Length and/or weight (if possible, obtain without stressing your pet)
- Food eaten
- Medicines or vitamin supplements given
- Shedding skin/molts – when and how often
- Toilet habits
- Breeding details – mating, births, egg laying, etc.

Record Card

Species _____   Male/Female _____

Name _____   Age _____

Date purchased _____   Preferred foods _____
_____

Length _____   _____

Date	Time	Event	Notes
e.g. for a Bearded Dragon			
October 10	noon	fed	8 crickets eaten. 12 left in vivarium.
October 11	morning	fed	A couple of crickets and some watercress eaten. Stalked one and captured it after 5 minutes.
October 12	morning	molt	Started shedding today. Sprayed him a lot. He rubbed himself on the wet cork and his old skin has started coming off.

Lizards Quiz

How well do you know your lizard?

Test your knowledge with the quiz below.

1. Which popular and easy-to-keep lizard selects and regularly uses one area of its vivarium as a toilet?

2. What term is used to describe the throat fan found on lizards such as iguanas and anoles?

3. What major survival function is provided by the Leopard Gecko's plump tail?

4. Do lizards have backbones?

5. Do all lizards have legs?

6. Which lizard is called a Jesus lizard, and why?

7. What is the world's largest known species of lizard?

8. A diurnal lizard does which of the following?
a. Sleeps in a cave.
b. Eats only flowers.
c. Is active during daylight hours.

9. Reptiles are more commonly found in tropical climates than temperate ones. True or False?

10. What do you eat if you are considered an omnivore?

11. Which terrestrial Australian lizard enjoys eating snails?

Answers

1. Leopard Gecko. 2. Dewlap. 3. It acts as a fat store and helps the lizard to survive periods of drought or when food and water are scarce. 4. Yes. 5. No, many do not. One legless European lizard is called the Slow Worm. 6. The Plumed Basilisk. This is because it has the amazing ability to run across open stretches of water. 7. The Komodo Dragon, which grows to 10 ft (3 m) in length. 8. c. 9. True. 10. A combination of plants and animals. 11. The Blue-tongued Skink.

Useful Information

There are a growing number of societies and local clubs that you may wish to join. They are a good source of information about all aspects of natural history and the maintenance of herptiles (reptiles and amphibians). They are also a good way of contacting like-minded individuals and obtaining livestock. Many reptile shows, which are open to the public, are advertised in their journals and newsletters.

Societies to join

International clubs and societies with interests in particular lizard families also abound. Many have their own informative newsletters and bulletins. Among others are:

The International Gecko Society
P.O. Box 370423
San Diego, CA 92137-0423

The Chameleon Information Network
13419 Appalachian Way
San Diego, CA 92129

Varanid Information Exchange
8726D South Sepulveda Blvd. #243
Los Angeles, CA 90045

Magazines and journals

The following magazines and journals are just a few examples of the periodicals available through subscription, pet shops, or on newsstands:

Reptile and Amphibian
An excellent journal currently produced monthly. Subscriptions are available from *Reptile and Amphibian Hobbyist*, One TFH Plaza, Neptune City, NJ 07753.

Reptiles
A larger-format monthly magazine dedicated primarily to herpetoculture and conservation. Subscription information may be obtained from *Reptiles* Magazine, P.O. Box 6050, Mission Viejo, CA 92690-6050

The Vivarium
The publication of the American Federation of Herpetoculturists (AFH), bimonthly and of large format. It is available by membership in the AFH, P.O. Box 300067, Escondido, CA 92030-0067.

Herp Review and the *Journal of Herpetology*
The Society for the Study of Reptiles and Amphibians (SSRA) publishes a nontechnical periodical, *Herb Review*, and the more scholarly *Journal of Herpetology*. Subscriptions are available from SSRA, Department of Zoology, Miami University, Oxford, OH 45056.

Copeia
The American Society of Ichthyologists and Herpetologists (ASIH) publishes *Copeia*, a technical journal that includes reptiles, amphibians, and fish. Subscription information is available from ASIH, Department of Zoology, Southern Illinois University, Carbondale, IL 62901-6501.

Books

R. D. Bartlett and Patricia Bartlett, *Chameleons, A Complete Pet Owner's Manual.* Hauppauge, NY: Barron's Educational Series, Inc., 1995.

R. D. Bartlett and Patricia Bartlett, *Lizard Care A–Z.* Hauppauge, NY: Barron's Educational Series, Inc., 1997.

G. M. Burghardt and A. S. Rand (Eds.), *Iguanas of the World: Their Behavior, Ecology, and Conservation.* Park Ridge, NJ: Noyes Publishing, 1982.
This very informative and scholarly volume, currently out of print, will soon be reissued by Krieger Publishing.

Fredric L. Frye, *Husbandry, Medicine, and Surgery in Captive Reptiles*, 2nd Ed. Malabar, FL: R. E. Krieger Publ. Co., 1991.

Index